# RUDE RHYMING SL

**compiled by Tom Nind**

**ABSON BOOKS LONDON** 5 Sidney Square London E1 2EY
Tel 020 7790 4737  Fax 020 7790 7346
email absonbooks@aol.com

**Abson Books London**
First published June 2003
5th impression March 2005
Cover design Chris Bird

Printed by Gutenberg Press, Malta
ISBN 0 902920 83 9

# CONTENTS

# PREFACE

Unlike the origins of Rhyming Cockney Slang, rude rhyming slang doesn't exist to prevent understanding or hide meaning but came into being simply to give the user the chance to express himself in a more colourful way.

Amongst the smut and filth contained within these pages, readers will be happy to discover nine different words for piles and haemorrhoids – together with more familiar terms such as Tommy Guns, Banana Splits and Andy Capp.

Some readers may feel that a kick in the Tom Doolies is a bit of a Tommy Tucker and can leave a fellow feeling Tom & Dick. Others will know, as they place their Tom Thumb on the Kermit the Frog for a Tom Tit, with a nasty case of the Tommy Guns, that it's not going to be their day. (Some will regret being called Tom in the first place.)

There will be many favourite phrases not included and hundreds yet to be invented but, whatever your reasons for reading this sordid little publication, brace yourself for some scatological revelations.

My thanks to all those who helped compile this book and particularly my mother – who was surprisingly knowledgeable.

*Tom*

# RUDE RHYMING SLANG – ENGLISH

| | |
|---|---|
| **Adam & the Ants** | pants |
| **Andy Capp** | crap |
| **Alan Whickers** | knickers |
| **Ali Oop** | poop |
| **Alphonse** | ponce |
| **Anthony Blunt** | cunt |
| **Auntie Annie** | fanny |

| | |
|---|---|
| **Bacon bits** | tits |
| **Bacon & eggs** | legs |

| | | | |
|---|---|---|---|
| **Banana splits** | shits | **Brian Clough** | rough |
| **Bangers & mash** | slash | **Brighton pier** | queer |
| **Barclays bank** | wank | **Brighton rock** | cock |
| **Barry White** | shite | **Bristol cities** | titties |
| **Basil Brush** | thrush | **Bubble & squeak** | leak |
| **Berkley Hunt** | cunt | | |
| **Berkshire Hunt** | cunt | | |
| **Berlin Walls** | balls | | |
| **Billy Hunt** | cunt | | |
| **Bill Wyman** | hymen | **C & A** | gay |
| **Black & Decker** | pecker | **Café au lait** | gay |
| **Blood red** (lipstick) | head (fellatio) | **Camels hump** | dump |
| **Boat & oar** | whore | **Carpet & rugs** | jugs |
| **Bob Cryer** | liar | **Casablanca** | wanker |
| **Brad Pitts** | tits/shits | **Cattle truck** | fuck |

## C

| | |
|---|---|
| **Chalfont St Giles** | piles |
| **Charlie Nash** | slash |
| **Chicken Oriental** | mental |
| **Christopher Lee** | pee |
| **Clark Kent** | bent |
| **Clement Freuds** | haemorrhoids |
| **Cloven hoofter** | poofter |
| **Cobblers awls** | balls |
| **Council gritter** | shitter |
| **Cream crackered** | knackered |
| **Cribbage pegs** | legs |

| | |
|---|---|
| **Deaf & dumb** | bum |
| **Diana Dors** | drawers |
| **Dickory Dock** | cock |
| **Divine Brown** | go down |
| **Donald Duck** | fuck |
| **Donald Trump** | hump |
| **Doris Day** | gay |
| **Doug McClure** | whore |
| **Douglas Hurd** | turd |
| **Dribs & drabs** | crabs |
| **Dukes of Argyles** | piles |

| | |
|---|---|
| **Ear of corn** | horn |
| **Eartha Kitt** | shit |
| **Eartha Kitts** | tits/shits |
| **Eddie Grundies** | undies |
| **Edinburgh Fringe** | minge |
| **Elephant & Castle** | arsehole |
| **Elephant's trunk** | spunk |
| **Elizabeth Regina** | vagina |
| **Emma Freuds** | haemorrhoids |

| | |
|---|---|
| **Farmer Giles** | piles |
| **Feather plucker** | fucker |
| **Fillet of cod** | sod |
| **Filter tips** | lips |
| **Fine & dandy** | randy |
| **Fish & shrimp** | pimp |
| **Fleas & ants** | pants |
| **Flying duck** | fuck |
| **Forrest Gump** | dump |
| **Four by four** | whore |
| **Frankie Vaughn** | porn |
| **Friar Tuck** | fuck |
| **Fun & frolics** | bollocks |

**g**

| | |
|---|---|
| **Gary Glitter** | shitter |
| **General Election** | erection |
| **General Smuts** | nuts |
| **George Best** | breast |
| **George Michael** | menstrual cycle |
| **George the Third** | turd |
| **Gigglestick** | prick |
| **Ginger beer** | queer |
| **Gobstopper** | chopper |
| **Grumble & grunt** | cunt |
| **Gypsies kiss** | piss |
| **Gypsy Rose Lee** | pee |

**h**

| | |
|---|---|
| **Ham & eggs** | legs |
| **Hampton Wick** | dick |
| **Harry Monk** | spunk |
| **Hat & cap** | clap (VD) |
| **Henry the Third** | turd |
| **Herring & kipper** | stripper |
| **Hit & miss** | kiss/piss |
| **Holy friar** | liar |
| **Horse & cart** | fart |
| **Howards Way** | gay |

**I**

| | |
|---|---|
| **Iron hoof** | poof |
| **Iron tank** | wank |

**J**

| | |
|---|---|
| **J. Arthur Rank** | wank |
| **Jack & Danny** | fanny |
| **Jack in the box** | pox |
| **Jack the Ripper** | stripper |
| **Jackson Pollocks** | bollocks |
| **Jacobs crackers** | knackers |
| **Jam roll** | arsehole |
| **James Hunt** | cunt |

| | |
|---|---|
| **Jimmy Riddle** | piddle |
| **Jimmy White** | shite |
| **Jodrell Bank** | wank |
| **John O'Groats** | oats |
| **John Woo** | poo |
| **Johnnie Cash** | slash |
| **Joystick** | prick |
| **Julian Clary** | fairy |

| | |
|---|---|
| **Kermit the frog** | bog |
| **Khyber Pass** | arse |
| **King Cole** | arsehole |

| King Lear | queer |
|-----------|-------|
| Kingdom come | dumb |
| Kuwaiti tanker | wanker |

## L

| Lamb shanks | wanks |
|-------------|-------|
| Light & bitter | shitter |
| Lionel Bart | fart |
| Lionel Richie | bitchy |
| Lolly lick | dick |
| London taxi | jacksie |
| Long & flexy | sexy |
| Lord Mayor | swear |

## M

| Mae West | breast |
|----------|--------|
| Magnus Pike | dyke |
| Maria Monk | spunk |
| Mark Ramprakash | slash |
| Mars & Venus | penis |
| Martin Chuzzlewit | shit |
| Mary Ellens | melons |
| Melvyn Bragg | shag/slag |
| Merchant banker | wanker |
| Metal Mickey | sickie |
| Metric miles | piles |
| Mickey Bliss | piss |
| Midland Bank | wank |

| | |
|---|---|
| **Mince tart** | fart |
| **Miss Fitch** | bitch |
| **Moby Dick** | sick |
| **Mods & Rockers** | knockers |
| **Molly O'Morgan** | organ |
| **Monkey wrench** | wench |
| **Mork & Mindy** | windy |
| **Morris Minor** | vagina |
| **Mystic Megs** | legs |

| | |
|---|---|
| **Niagara Falls** | balls |
| **Nick Cotton** | rotten |
| **Nobby Stiles** | piles |
| **Nuremberg Trials** | piles |

| | |
|---|---|
| **Oedipus Rex** | sex |
| **Oliver Twist** | pissed |
| **Orange & pear** | swear |
| **Orchestra stalls** | balls |

**Pat Cash** slash
**Pat & Mick** sick
**Peddle & crank** wank
**Pedigree Chum** cum
**Perry Como** homo
**Peters & Lee** pee
**Pheasant plucker** fucker
**Pipe & drum** bum/cum
**Polo Mint** bint
**Pony & trap** crap
**Popcorn** horn
**Pork pies** lies

**Port & brandy** randy
**Posh & Becks** sex
**Push the truck** fuck

**Queen Mum** bum

**Rabbit hutch** crutch
**Racquel Welch** belch
**Radio Ones** runs

| | |
|---|---|
| **Radio Rental** | mental |
| **Rag & bone** | throne (WC) |
| **Raspberry ripple** | nipple |
| **Raspberry tart** | fart |
| **Ravi Shankar** | wanker |
| **Reggie & Ronnie**(Kray) | Johnnie |
| **Richard The Third** | turd/bird |
| **Rip Van Winkle** | tinkle |
| **Roger Moore** | whore |
| **Ronson lighter** | shiter |
| **Royal Albert Halls** | balls |
| **Rubber duck** | fuck |
| **Rubik's cube** | pube |
| **Rusty Spike** | dyke |

| | |
|---|---|
| **Saint Moritz** | tits/shits |
| **Sammy Lee** | pee |
| **Sandy McNabs** | crabs |
| **Santa's Grotto** | blotto |
| **Scotch eggs** | legs |
| **Scotch mist** | pissed |
| **Shabba Ranks** | wanks |
| **Sherman tank** | wank |
| **Ships anchor** | wanker |
| **Sieg Heils** | piles |
| **Sigourney Weaver** | beaver |
| **Spam fritter** | shitter |
| **Sri Lanker** | wanker |

| | | | |
|---|---|---|---|
| **Stick of rock** | cock | **Three card trick** | dick |
| **Stoke on Trent** | bent | **Three wheel trike** | dyke |
| **Strawberry spilt** | git | **Threepenny bits** | tits |
| **Sue Ellens** | melons | **Tilbury Dock** | cock |
| **Sylvester Stallone** | bone | **Tin roof** | poof |
| | | **Tom & Dick** | sick |
| | | **Tom Doolies** | goolies |
| | | **Tom Kite** | shite |
| | | **Tom Tit** | shit |
| **T Rex** | sex | **Tom Thumb** | bum |
| **Terry Scotts** | trots | **Tommy Tucker** | fucker |
| **That & this** | piss | **Tommy guns** | runs |
| **Thelonius Monk** | spunk | **Tung Chee Hwa** | bra |
| **Thespian** | lesbian | **Turkish delight** | shite |
| **Thomas More** | whore | **Two bob bits** | shits |

**Uncle Bob**    knob
**Uncle Dick**    sick
**Uncle Silly**    willy

**Von Trapp**    crap

**Wallace & Gromit**    vomit
**Walter Mitty**    titty
**Watford Gap**    crap
**Whiplash**    slash
**Willy Wonka**    plonker
**Wyatt Earp**    burp

**Zorba the Greek**    leak

# ENGLISH – RUDE RHYMING SLANG

# a

**Arse**      Khyber Pass

**Arsehole**     Elephant & Castle

jam roll

King Cole

# b

**Balls**      Berlin Walls

cobblers awls

Niagara Falls

orchestra stalls

Royal Albert Halls

**Beaver**     Sigourney Weaver

| **Belch** | Racquel Welch |
| **Bent** | Clark Kent |
| | Stoke-on-Trent |
| **Bint** | Polo Mint |
| **Bird** | Richard the Third |
| **Bitch** | Miss Fitch |
| **Bitchy** | Lionel Richie |
| **Blotto** | Santa's grotto |
| **Bog** | Kermit the frog |
| **Bollocks** | fun & frolics |
| | Jackson Pollocks |
| **Bone** | Sylvester Stallone |
| **Bra** | Tung Chee Hwa |
| **Breast** | Mae West |
| | George Best |

| **Bum** | deaf & dumb |
| | pipe & drum |
| | Queen Mum |
| | Tom Thumb |
| **Burp** | Wyatt Earp |

# C

| **Chopper** | gobstopper |
| **Clap** (VD) | hat & cap |
| **Cock** | Brighton rock |
| | Dickory Dock |
| | stick of rock |
| | Tilbury Dock |

| | | | |
|---|---|---|---|
| **Crabs** | dribs & drabs | | |
| | Sandy McNabs | **d** | |
| **Crap** | Andy Capp | **Dick** | Hampton Wick |
| | pony & trap | | lolly lick |
| | Von Trapp | | three card trick |
| | Watford Gap | **Drawers** | Diana Dors |
| **Crutch** | rabbit hutch | **Dumb** | kingdom come |
| **Cum** | Pedigree Chum | **Dump** | camels hump |
| | pipe & drum | | Forrest Gump |
| **Cunt** | Anthony Blunt | **Dyke** | Magnus Pike |
| | Berkley Hunt | | rusty spike |
| | Berkshire Hunt | | three wheel trike |
| | Billy Hunt | | |
| | grumble & grunt | | |
| | James Hunt | | |

# e

**Erection**    General Election

# f

**Fairy**    Julian Clary
**Fanny**    Auntie Annie
            Jack & Danny
**Fart**    horse & cart
            Lionel Bart
            mince tart
            raspberry tart
**Fuck**    cattle truck

**Fucker**    Donald Duck
            flying duck
            Friar Tuck
            push the truck
            rubber duck
            feather plucker
            pheasant plucker
            Tommy Tucker

# g

**Gay**    C & A
            Café au lait
            Doris Day
            Howards Way

| Git | strawberry split |
| Go down | Divine Brown |
| Goolies | Tom Doolies |

## h

| Head (fellatio) | blood red (lipstick) |
| Haemorrhoids | Clement Freuds |
| | Emma Freuds |
| Homo | Perry Como |
| Horn | ear of corn |
| | popcorn |
| Hump | Donald Trump |
| Hymen | Bill Wyman |

| Jacksie | London taxi |
| Johnny | Reggie & Ronnie (Kray) |
| Jugs | carpet & rugs |

## k

| Kiss | hit & miss |
| Knackered | cream crackered |
| Knackers | Jacobs Crackers |
| Knickers | Alan Whickers |
| Knockers | Mods & Rockers |
| Knob | Uncle Bob |

# l

| | |
|---|---|
| **Leak** | bubble & squeak |
| | Zorba the Greek |
| **Legs** | bacon & eggs |
| | cribbage pegs |
| | ham & eggs |
| | Mystic Megs |
| | scotch eggs |
| **Lesbian** | Thespian |
| **Liar** | Bob Cryer |
| | Holy Friar |
| **Lies** | pork pies |
| **Lips** | filter tips |

# m

| | |
|---|---|
| **Melons** | Mary Ellens |
| | Sue Ellens |
| **Mental** | chicken oriental |
| | Radio Rental |
| **Menstrual cycle** | George Michael |
| **Minge** | Edinburgh Fringe |

# n

| | |
|---|---|
| **Nipple** | Raspberry Ripple |
| **Nuts** | General Smuts |

# O

**Oats** John O'Groats

**Organ** Molly O'Morgan

# p

**Pants** Adam & the Ants
fleas & ants

**Pecker** Black & Decker

**Pee** Christopher Lee
Gypsy Rose Lee
Peters & Lee
Sammy Lee

**Penis** Mars & Venus

**Piddle** Jimmy Riddle

**Piles** Chalfont St Giles
Dukes of Argyles
Farmer Giles
metric miles
Nobby Stiles
Nuremberg Trials
Sieg Heils

**Pimp** fish & shrimp

**Piss** gypsies kiss
hit & miss
Mickey Bliss
that & this

**Pissed** Oliver Twist

|          | Scotch mist        |
|----------|--------------------|
| **Plonker** | Willy Wonka      |
| **Ponce**   | Alphonse         |
| **Poo**     | John Woo         |
| **Poof**    | iron hoof        |
|          | tin roof           |
| **Poofter** | cloven hoofter   |
| **Poop**    | Ali Oop          |
| **Porn**    | Frankie Vaughn   |
| **Pox**     | Jack in the box  |
| **Prick**   | gigglestick      |
|          | joystick           |
| **Pube**    | Rubik's Cube     |

# q

| **Queer** | Brighton Pier |
|-----------|---------------|
|           | ginger beer   |
|           | King Lear     |

# r

| **Randy**  | fine & dandy   |
|------------|----------------|
|            | port & brandy  |
| **Rotton** | Nick Cotton    |
| **Rough**  | Brian Clough   |
| **Runs**   | Radio Ones     |
|            | Tommy Guns     |

# S

| | |
|---|---|
| **Sex** | Oedipus Rex |
| | Posh & Becks |
| | T Rex |
| **Sexy** | long & flexy |
| **Shag** | Melvyn Bragg |
| **Shit** | Martin Chuzzlewit |
| | Tom Tit |
| | Eartha Kitt |
| **Shite** | Barry White |
| | Jimmy White |
| | Tom Kite |
| | Turkish Delight |
| **Shiter** | Ronson lighter |
| **Shits** | banana splits |
| | Brad Pitts |
| | Earth Kitts |
| | San Moritz |
| | two bob bits |
| **Shitter** | council gritter |
| | Gary Glitter |
| | light & bitter |
| | spam fritter |
| **Sick** | Moby Dick |
| | Pat & Mick |
| | Tom & Dick |
| | Uncle Dick |
| **Sickie** | Metal Mickey |
| **Slag** | Melvyn Bragg |

| **Slash** | bangers & mash |
| | Charlie Nash |
| | Johnnie Cash |
| | Mark Ramprakash |
| | Pat Cash |
| | whiplash |
| **Sod** | fillet of cod |
| **Spunk** | elephant's trunk |
| | Harry Monk |
| | Maria Monk |
| | Thelonius Monk |
| **Stripper** | herring & kipper |
| | Jack the Ripper |
| **Swear** | Lord Mayor |
| | orange & pear |

t

| **Throne** (wc) | rag & bone |
| **Thrush** | Basil Brush |
| **Tinkle** | Rip Van Winkle |
| **Titties** | Bristol Cities |
| **Tits** | bacon bits |
| | Brad Pitts |
| | Saint Moritz |
| | threepenny bits |
| | Eartha Kitts |
| **Titty** | Walter Mitty |
| **Trots** | Terry Scotts |
| **Turd** | Douglas Hurd |
| | Richard the Third |

George the Third
Henry the Third

# U
**Undies**

Eddie Grundies

# V
**Vagina**

Elizabeth Regina
Morris Minor

**Vomit**

Wallace & Gromit

# W
**Wank**

Barclays Bank
iron tank
J Arthur Rank
Jodrell Bank
Midland Bank
peddle & crank
Sherman tank

**Wanker**

Casablanca
Kuwaiti tanker
merchant banker
Ravi Shankar
ships anchor
Sri Lanka

| **Wanks** | lamb shanks |
|-----------|-------------|
|           | Shabba Ranks |
| **Wench** | monkey wrench |
| **Whore** | boat & oar |
|           | Doug McClure |
|           | four by four |
|           | Roger Moore |
|           | Thomas More |
| **Willy** | Uncle Silly |
| **Windy** | Mork & Mindy |

# OTHER TITLES AVAILABLE

*Language Glossaries*

**American English/English American**

**Australian English/English Australian**

**Irish English/English Irish**

**Gay Slang**

**Geordie English**

**Lancashire English**

**Prison Slang**

**Rhyming Cockney Slang**

**Scouse English**

**Yiddish English/English Yiddish**

**Scottish English/English Scottish**

**Yorkshire English**

**Ultimate Language of Flowers**

**Hip Hop English**

**The Death of Kings**
(A medical history of the Kings &
Queens of England)

*Literary Quiz & Puzzle Books*

**Jane Austen**

**Brontë Sisters**

**Charles Dickens**

**Gilbert & Sullivan**

**Thomas Hardy**

**Sherlock Holmes**

**Shakespeare**

All of these titles are available from good booksellers or by contacting the publisher:

**Abson Books London**
5 Sidney Square London E1 2EY
Tel 020 7790 4737
Fax 020 7790 7346
email absonbooks@aol.com
Web: www.absonbooks.co.uk